On t[illegible]ent

Examining the Debates on Christ's Reconciling Work

Oliver D Crisp
Principal of St Mary's College and
Head of the School of Divinity, University of St Andrews

GROVE BOOKS LIMITED
RIDLEY HALL RD CAMBRIDGE CB3 9HU

Contents

Acknowledgments

The author would like to thank the following individuals for their assistance in the production of this text: Professor Mike Higton, the Rev'd Dr Jared Michelson and Danielle Ross. Dr Joanna Leidenhag persuaded the author to write this work. It is to be hoped that the result does not give her cause to regret her decision.

First Impression August 2022
ISSN 2633-8394
ISBN 978 1 78827 259 9

1

Introduction

According to Qoheleth, of the making of many books there is no end, and much study is wearisome to the flesh (Eccl 12.12).[1] If that is right, then it seems appropriate to begin yet another work on the atonement—even if it is a short introductory work—with the question, 'Why?' That is, why do we need another treatment of this topic? Are not there already enough published works on the subject?

The answer to that question is, in a sense, a way of addressing Qoheleth's pithy remark as well. There are indeed many books on this topic, including many good books. But work on the atonement continues apace, and there has been a renewed interest in the doctrine in recent Christian theology from biblical studies, historical, systematic and analytic theologians, as well as pastors and homileticians (see, for example, the monumental work of Fleming Rutledge in this regard).[2] So it seems appropriate to have a work such as this one to help students and lay people interested in this central doctrine to navigate their way through what one recent author on the topic has called the 'maze' of views on Christ's reconciling work.[3]

There has been a renewed interest in the atonement in recent Christian theology

To that end, this is a short introduction to some of the main issues in the atonement. It is not a comprehensive treatment of the matter. (How could it be?) But it should provide some orientation. Interested readers not too wearied in their flesh by the consideration of what follows may pursue matters further by consulting the Further Reading at the end of this booklet.

We shall proceed as follows. Chapter two considers the question, 'What is the atonement?' If this is in fact a central doctrine in Christian teaching, what is it and what does it mean? Often theologians use technical terms in addressing this question. In the course of setting out what the atonement is, I shall introduce several of the most important of these, explaining them as we go along. Chapter three sets out the distinction between Christ's person and work. Here I will argue that a complete account of Christ's work of reconciliation must include his incarnation, ministry, and death and resurrection. Chapter four gives a brief overview of some historic accounts of the atonement, including some patristic views, some medieval views, and some early modern and more recent views. The focus is on giving a brief and sympathetic account of the internal logic and structure of each particular understanding of the atonement, *eg* ransom, substitution, satisfaction and so on—terms that will become clear as we proceed. Chapter five turns to consider one more view of atonement that draws on these previous ideas, as well as recent work on the Pauline notion of participation in the reconciling work of Christ. This is called the *representational account*. The essay ends with a brief conclusion, which draws together the substance of what has been previously said.

What is the Atonement?

2

Often, the atonement is said to be the doctrine according to which Christ brings about reconciliation between fallen human beings and Godself. The divine saving work results in an *at-one-ment*. Hence the name. This is helpful as far as it goes. *Atonement* is an odd English word that does not really have an equivalent in the biblical traditions. But it does capture the idea, central in much of the biblical material, that Christ is the means by which we are brought back into renewed relationship with God. And that, it seems to me, is what the atonement is all about.

We need reconciling because, on at least one traditional way of thinking about the matter, we are estranged from God as a consequence of our sin. There are other ways of thinking about the reason for the atonement. But the idea that we need Christ to save us from our sins is the most common one, and can be traced back to the biblical witness.[4] As the writer of the pastoral epistles puts it, 'The saying is sure and worthy of full acceptance, that Christ Jesus came into the world to save sinners' (1 Tim 1.15). It does not get much more direct than that. So what brings about such estrangements from God? The story goes something like this. Our aboriginal parents who enjoyed unbroken communion with their creator sinned by eating the fruit of the tree of the knowledge of good and evil, thereby disrupting their relationship with God and bringing about a deep moral and legal cleft between themselves and their creator, as well as their progeny. This primeval transgression resulted in a disordering of human beings thereafter, so that we are generated in a morally broken state because of the primal sin of our ancestors. As a result, we are incapable of pleasing God without some interposition of divine grace. What is more, if we live long enough, we will end up sinning for ourselves because of the sinful predisposition with which we are formed. (The biblical backstory to this narrative can be found in Genesis 1–3, Rom 5.12–19 and 1 Cor 15.)[5]

We are incapable of pleasing God without some interposition of divine grace

Understandings of the Atonement

Christian communities down through the centuries have understood this narrative about human estrangement from God rather differently, resulting in diverging accounts of the nature of the broken relationship and its seriousness.

(The discerning reader will have noted that my retelling of the story betrays my own Protestant heritage in this regard.) For some Christians, the mistake made by our first parents wounded the nature borne by human beings, such that we are now generated with that wound, though it may be healed given the right divine treatment. This is the way in which many Eastern Orthodox Christians think about the matter. As a consequence, they eschew language of original sin to describe the putative condition that we all bear as a consequence of Adam's primal sin, preferring instead to speak of the *ancestral sin* that leaves this wound.[6] Roman Catholic Christians have tended to speak in terms of a privation as well, but in more robust moral categories than the Eastern Orthodox, and including a notion of original sin as a moral condition that results from a primeval fall. What we lose in the primeval fall, according to Roman Catholic theology, is *original justice*—a state of moral order that was enjoyed by our first parents, but which was withdrawn upon committing the primal sin.[7] Protestants have tended to speak in stronger terms still. As Article 9 of the *Articles of Religion* (1571) puts it:

> Original Sin standeth not in the following of Adam, (as the Pelagians do vainly talk;) but it is the fault and corruption of the Nature of every man, that naturally is ingendered of the offspring of Adam; whereby man is very far gone from original righteousness, and is of his own nature inclined to evil, so that the flesh lusteth always contrary to the spirit; and therefore in every person born into this world, it deserveth God's wrath and damnation.

This is fairly strong stuff. Later Protestant theology, especially in the Reformed tradition, made a clear distinction between *original sin* as the moral corruption with which we are all generated *in utero*, and *original guilt*, the culpability for Adam's sin that is included alongside original sin itself. This is even stronger still. However, not all Protestant Christians have observed this distinction. (Among the Magisterial Reformers, neither Huldrych Zwingli in Zurich, nor John Calvin in Geneva, made this distinction).[8]

Reconciling Humanity

Whether we think of the sin that affects human beings as a wound, as a state of privation (lacking the original justice with which Adam and Eve were supposedly created), or as a state of moral corruption (perhaps including guilt for that corruption), the point is that human beings are in a state of sin. All have sinned and fall short of the glory of God (Rom 3.23). Yet, 'they are now justified by his grace as a gift, through the redemption that is in Christ Jesus' (Rom 3.24). So in one traditional way of understanding atonement, it is the doctrine according to which Christ brings about reconciliation for all fallen human beings—by which is meant all human beings who are estranged from God as a consequence of being a sinner in a state of sin, however this is understood.

When discussing the doctrine of atonement a further helpful distinction can be made between the nature of the atonement (*what it is*), and the scope of atonement (*who it saves*). In this booklet I will be concerned mainly with the nature of the atonement, not the scope of atonement. By the nature of atonement, I mean the mechanism by means of which human beings may be reconciled to Godself. Put differently, we might ask: 'How is it that Christ saves fallen human beings from their sin?' The answer to this question will involve thinking about what it is that Christ does that brings about human reconciliation with God. In a similar way, when someone asks, 'How does the grandfather clock in the hallway actually work?' they are asking about what goes on inside the clock. What is it that makes it work—what is the mechanism involved? We are asking a similar question of the atonement when we ask about its nature. But we could ask a slightly different question. This second question is not about how the atonement works (to the extent that we finite human beings can understand such a divine mystery) but rather, for whom does Christ die? Who is saved by his reconciling work? Is it some people, those who believe perhaps? Is it many people, few people—*all* people? Whatever answer we give to this question, it should be clear that it is distinct from the question of the mechanism of atonement. In this latter case, we are interested in the *scope* of Christ's saving work, just as we might worry about how many people a particular batch of vaccine may save.

Different Types of Reflection

A third sort of distinction relevant to our purposes has to do with what it is that our reflection on atonement may achieve. We might distinguish between a doctrine, a dogma, a motif, a model, theories and mysteries.

In my way of thinking, a doctrine is *a comprehensive account of a particular teaching about a given theological topic held by some community of Christians or some particular denomination*.[9] An example would be the historic two natures doctrine of the incarnation, according to which Christ is one person subsisting in two natures: one divine, the other human. The atonement is another such doctrine. Of course, there are different doctrines on particular theological topics held by different communions and groups down through the centuries. So we will have to bear this in mind. Our doctrines are often rather fragile things. We may get doctrine wrong. So we should bear with one another as we think about the deep mysteries of the Christian faith like the atonement. Perhaps it may turn out that our own doctrines need to be finessed by attending to what other people have said on the matter.

For present purposes, a dogma is a particular kind of doctrine, one that has a formal definition or a particular shape given to it by a particular church or communion. In Roman Catholic teaching a dogma is defined by the Magisterium, that is, the teaching office of the church. Protestants have no such body, but there are confessions and creeds that most Protestants observe, and that have a similar role. One such is the Thirty-nine Articles; another would be the Westminster Confession, which was originally conceived as a revision to the Thirty-nine Articles. We might think of the sort of doctrines set forth in these official documents of particular Protestant communions as dogma in this sense.

A motif is a kind of theme, like a leitmotif in a piece of orchestral music that is an important theme that crops up repeatedly through the piece of music as a kind of refrain. We shall see that in atonement theology there are motifs and themes, some of which are aspects of larger models or doctrines of atonement, but some of which are not. This is important when it comes to assessing whether a particular account of the atonement is actually *more* than a motif or theme, and amounts to a complete doctrine or account of Christ's reconciling work.

A model is a rather different thing. It is a kind of conceptual picture, a simplified description of more complex data. An example of what I mean would be the picture of an atom that can be found in many physics textbooks. No one has seen an atom. But the picture in the textbook helps us get a conceptual grip on it. It provides a picture for us that helps us understand some of its properties even if, strictly speaking, the atom does not look exactly like the picture in the book. Similarly, in Christian theology we can produce models for thinking about doctrine—conceptual pictures that help us get a better purchase on what we are talking about. We shall see that there are many such models in historic discussion of the atonement. Models are revisable and fallible. But they are helpful too. They often contain or include metaphors, like 'the Lamb of God.' Metaphors are tropes that have a superabundance of meaning. Christ is a lamb in a way similar to the lamb scarified on Passover. He is the sacrifice for our sin. He is spotless and without sin. He is God's lamb, being God's messenger to us. He is also (somehow) both God himself and a creature...and so on. Some theologians have claimed that all model language in theology is just grand metaphor.[10] I am not persuaded by this, though I think that metaphor plays an important role in theology, and especially in discussion of the atonement.

Metaphor plays an important role in theology, especially in the atonement

Sometimes, especially in older, Victorian-era textbooks on the atonement, one finds discussion of various *theories* of atonement.[11] I shall refrain from such language here for the most part. That is because I do not think we have theories of atonement. What we have are usually motifs, doctrines and models of atonement. A theory is something more grand than these things. It gives us a complete conceptual account of a given thing, like the theory of general or special relativity in physics. But particular Christian doctrines are not usually like this. They are at best simplified descriptions of complex data, that is, conceptual pictures that help us to apprehend something—but not everything—about the great mystery of salvation that is given to us in Christ.

Finally, I have mentioned the word 'mystery' several times already. By a mystery, I mean something, whether some notion or some entity, which is beyond our ken. Note, saying something is a mystery does not mean it is contradictory, or paradoxical, or meaningless. Far from it! A mystery is just something we limited human beings cannot fathom. There are many such mysteries in the world around us. Not all of them are theological. For instance, the mystery of how minds are related to bodies, or the mystery of how light behaves like particles under certain experimental conditions, and like waves under other experimental conditions. All the central doctrines in Christian theology are mysteries. We cannot fathom them. This should not be surprising since our knowledge of God and God's purposes depends in important respects upon God revealing Godself to us. Since God is beyond our ken, it is not surprising that much of what God reveals of God's purposes is baffling or difficult for us to comprehend. This includes central aspects of the atonement. At best, our theological reflection on this matter should help us get a better understanding of the faith we have been given. It will not provide us with a complete explanation of that faith.

All the central doctrines in Christian theology are mysteries

3 The Person and Work of Christ

Having considered some introductory matters about what the doctrine of atonement is concerned with, we can now turn to the question of the nature of the atonement. However, before we come to that it is important to register several theological distinctions. The first is between the person and work of Christ. The second is how Christ's work of reconciliation includes his incarnation, ministry and death, resurrection and session at the right hand of the Father in heaven. Let us consider these two sorts of distinction in turn.

It is possible in principle to differentiate between the person and work of Christ. His person is *who he is*: God the Son incarnate. His work is *what he does*: he becomes incarnate to reconcile fallen human beings to Godself. Thus his person is not to be confused with his work just as the person of the surgeon is not to be confused with their work as they attempt to operate on a patient. However, there is another sense in which the person and work of Christ are really of a piece. For the incarnation occurs because of human sin (recall 1 Tim 1.15). It may be that there are other reasons for the incarnation as well. (Perhaps we need a hub or interface between divinity and humanity in order to be united to God and be in a position to participate in the divine life. But that is a matter for another day.)

It seems fairly safe to say the incarnation is the beginning of the saving work of Christ in the economy of salvation. That is, in God's purposes, and according to passages like 1 Tim 1.15, Christ Jesus came into the world to save sinners. He became incarnate to do the work of reconciliation. In a similar manner, the surgeon went to medical school to be able to perform the life-saving procedures they do on a daily basis. They underwent a particular preparation to perform a certain kind of task. But is the incarnation merely *preparation* for the work of atonement? Can we keep the person of Christ and his work separate in this manner? Many historic Christian thinkers have denied that we can do so. Perhaps the most influential of these is the great theologian of the early church, Athanasius. In *On the Incarnation* he writes, 'He became man that we might become God.'[12] The idea here is not that God the Son becomes human so that we literally become divine. Rather, the idea is that God the Son becomes human so as to scoop up our humanity, and, by perfecting it,

God the Son becomes human so as to scoop up our humanity

enable us to be united to Godself once more in unbroken communion and participate in the divine life. It is as if God the Son enters our miserable state of sin, becoming human, in order to transform that humanity from the inside out. Through living a perfect life, and dying on our behalf and for our sake, he enters the state of death and destroys death itself—making possible new life through being resurrected from the dead and ascending into heaven to sit at the right hand of the Father. In other words, in Athanasius' expansive vision of salvation, the whole of the life and ministry, as well as the death, resurrection and ascension of Christ are included as different phases of his one work of reconciliation. On his way of thinking, Christ Jesus truly came into the world, becoming incarnate, in order to save sinners.

Not all theologians have seen things this way. As a counterpoint to Athanasius, consider the work of the medieval doctor of the church, Anselm of Canterbury. In his magisterial work *Cur deus homo*, or *Why the God Man*, he begins with the assumption that the incarnation was a kind of necessary condition for the work of atonement, but is not itself part of that act of atonement.[13] For atonement, according to Anselm, is what was brought about through the death of Christ on the cross. This way of thinking has been very influential in subsequent Western theology, especially in Protestant ways of thinking about the atonement. But with greatest respect to the sublime Anselm, I think he is mistaken in this regard. Athanasius seems to be tracking with the biblical tradition more closely in this matter. If that is right, then Christ's reconciling work is a much richer thing than much historic Protestant theology has supposed. For it includes his incarnation, life, ministry, death, resurrection and ascension—and, perhaps, his session at the right hand of the Father, where he intercedes for the saints (Rom 8.34; Hebrews 7). This is not to deny that the crucifixion and death of Christ is of fundamental theological importance, for the New Testament writers make that abundantly clear in their writings (see, for example, 1 Pet 3.18, or Rom 5). But it is to place this fundamental aspect of Christ's saving work into a broader context of salvation—one that includes his being made flesh, and living and ministering among fallen human beings as well as dying and rising and ascending into heaven.

4 The Nature of Atonement

Thus far, we have seen that Christ's atoning work is principally about the reconciliation of fallen human beings with God—for Christ Jesus came into the world to save sinners (1 Tim 1.15). According to theologians like Athanasius (and in modern times, theologians like Thomas Torrance, Kathryn Tanner and Ian McFarland who have followed the lead of Athanasius in this regard), he does this by means of his incarnation, life, death and resurrection.[14] The whole of Christ's life and work is one complex act of atonement with different phases or parts. Even if this seems plausible, it still leaves us with questions. For instance, how is it that Christ brings about human reconciliation by means of his incarnation, life, death and resurrection? What is it about these different things that, taken together, bring about human salvation?

There are many different answers to this question in the history of theology. One of the oft-repeated oddities about the atonement as a Christian doctrine is that it is both a central and defining teaching of the Christian faith, and yet also a doctrine that has no definite shape laid down in the ancient creeds of the church. The same is not true of, say, the Trinity or the incarnation—the two other obvious candidates for central and defining doctrines in Christianity. In the case of the Trinity we have the definition of the dogma in the Nicene-Constantinopolitan creed of AD 381. It is still the basis for the vast majority of Christian confession today. Similarly, in the case of the incarnation, we have the so-called Chalcedonian definition of the person of Christ, which was codified by the Fathers of the Council of Chalcedon in AD 451. They promulgated the teaching that Christ is one person subsisting in two natures, one divine and the other human. This has passed down to us as the *two natures doctrine,* and is a touchstone for rightly understanding the person of Christ. No such dogmatic statement is to be had about the atonement. For this reason, different accounts of atonement abound, usually drawing on one or more motif or metaphor to be found in the biblical witness.

Moral Example

One common idea about atonement is that it is an example of God's love for us. This is sometimes called the *moral exemplar view.* On this way of thinking, Christ's atonement is an expression of divine love, an indication of how much God cares for fallen humanity that he would send the Son to die for humanity.

Stated like this, the view is not very clear. Does it imply some mechanism of atonement in addition to divine love, or does it simply indicate that God loves us—and if it does, why do we need an atonement anyway? Surely God could simply demonstrate God's love in forgiving us our sin without atonement?

The moral example view could, in fact, be understood in one of several ways. This is not always made clear in the literature, which is one reason why it is one of the most misunderstood approaches to the atonement.[15] At one level, the moral exemplar view could simply be the idea that Christ's work is an example of God's love for us that we should imitate. In which case, there is nothing about this view that involves the reconciliation of fallen human beings to Godself, and the view is not, in fact, a doctrine of atonement. We might think of it as a way of understanding the work of Christ without thinking of it in terms of an atonement at all. Such a way of understanding moral exemplarism is in principle open to someone without specifically Christian commitments—such as someone who believes in a god, but not necessarily in all the accoutrements of Christianity. But a second way of thinking about the atonement as a moral example does amount to a doctrine of reconciliation. For suppose that someone reads the gospels or hears a sermon on Christ's passion, and is deeply moved by the example of God's love in the work of Christ. And suppose that this reading or this sermon is the occasion of a transformative experience in that person's life. They come to understand themselves as a child of God and as one loved by God in Christ, and so forth. This might bring about a profound and lasting change in the person concerned. This looks much more like an account of moral exemplarism which does amount to a doctrine of atonement.

But note too, that all Christian theologians of whatever stripe can affirm these two ways of thinking about Christ's work as a moral example. We might say that this way of thinking is a kind of bare minimum for a Christian understanding of the work of Christ as a reconciling work. However, most theologians have regarded it as insufficient on its own, and without further theological explanation of why going to a violent death is a loving act to be emulated. So one of the oddities of the moral example view is that although it may yield a conceptually thin account of Christ's work as an atonement, it is often thought to be only the first step to a more comprehensive or expansive way of thinking about how it is that Christ's work reconciles us to Godself.[16]

The moral example view yields a conceptually thin account of Christ's work as an atonement

Ransom

Next, let us consider the notion of ransom, and the idea that Christ somehow buys fallen human beings back from sin, death and the devil at the cost of his own life. There are biblical precedents for this in the use of the term, such as 1 Tim 2.6, which tells us that Christ gave himself as a ransom for all (the Greek word here is *lutron*). Similarly, in Heb 2.14–15 we read that Christ became human, 'so that through death he might destroy the one who has the power of death, that is, the devil, and free those who all their lives were held in slavery by the fear of death.' Here too, it is a ransom that seems to be in view. In modern theology this idea that Christ purchases fallen human beings at the cost of his own life has been joined to the idea of Christ as victor over sin, death and the devil. This is an ancient idea that goes back to early church fathers like Athanasius and Irenaeus (though they are not defenders of a ransom view of atonement as such).[17] But in more recent theology these two ideas have come apart. Some modern theologians, like the Anabaptist J Denny Weaver, speak of Christ's victory in atonement without a clear mechanism in view, and without assimilating his victory to the specific idea of ransom.[18]

Sacrifice

Another important metaphor is that of Christ as the sacrifice for human sin. There is a heated debate in certain theological circles about how to understand the terms propitiation and expiation as they have been used to translate the biblical terms *hilasterion* and *hilasmos*.[19] Expiation has to do with the removal of sin, whereas propitiation has to do with placating or appeasing someone. One worry raised by a number of theologians critical of traditional ways of understanding and translating these terms in the language of propitiation is that it implies God must be appeased or placated by the sacrifice of Christ's body. And this seems to raise serious questions about the divine character. For what sort of god requires sacrifice in order to be appeased? The language of expiation does not have the same connotations, and so is often thought to be a less objectionable way of translating the relevant Greek terms in the New Testament.

The divine character and life are not subject to change from without

I do not propose to enter into the intricate debates over these matters carried on by biblical scholars, important though they may be. Instead, I will simply say this: Christ's saving work certainly does remove our sin and culpability, and does provide us with a means by which to be reconciled to Godself. That, much Scripture and the majority voice in historic Christianity are united in affirming. But it is odd to think that God must be placated or appeased. God is not whimsical or subject to megrim. He does not require some human action in order to bring about our salvation. Nor is he emotionally mercurial. In fact, according to much traditional Christian theology, God is immutable in the sense that the divine character and life are not subject to change from without. That is, God is not perturbed by human action. The Deity is perfect in all his ways (Deut 32.4; 2 Sam 22.31; Ps 18.30; Jas 1.17). Thus, we should take care when interpreting images used in Scripture to describe God's action that are anthropomorphic or anthropopathic in nature, ascribing human states and actions to God. These images or concepts are metaphorical or analogous; they do not necessarily express things that can be directly and unproblematically mapped onto God's nature. Christ may remove human sin by his atonement (expiation). He may, in some circumstances, be said to appease or placate God (propitiation). But it is not obvious that we can derive from this the idea that God is essentially angry or wrathful, like some human parent; he is not. Nevertheless, God is just and the effects of divine justice may be seen in the way in which it is distributed in, say, the punishment of sin or its atonement (Ps 89.14; Isa 30.18).[20]

Satisfaction

This excursus on expiation and propitiation is important because they have informed motifs of satisfaction and penal substitution, two distinct but related accounts of the atonement. Satisfaction, which was first set forth in a systematic way by Anselm of Canterbury, is the idea that Christ's death is a supererogatory act that generates a merit. This merit God then accepts in lieu of the punishment for human sin that would otherwise be visited upon the guilty. Christ satisfies the honour of God that has been infringed by human sin, and that requires an appropriate act of recompense. But note that for those who defend this view, Christ's atonement is not a punishment. It is a meritorious act that is accepted instead of punishment. In fact, it is a meritorious act that is above and beyond the call of duty (which is what supererogation means). Christ is without sin and does not already owe all he is and has to God for any sin committed. So he can offer himself on behalf of sinful human beings to satisfy the debt they owe to God. He is able to provide a suitable satisfaction because the act of the God-human generates an infinite merit—for it is the act of God incarnate. Thus, satisfaction is offered by Christ, and the believer is united to Christ by faith and participation in the sacramental life of the church.

Penal Substitution

Penal substitution shares much in common with satisfaction, and looks to similar biblical roots. But it is a distinct way of thinking about atonement. According to the doctrine of penal substitution, Christ's death is a vicarious action that involves him being punished in the place of the sinner, or, in more moderate versions of the doctrine, involves him suffering the penal consequences of human sin.[21] Let me explain this difference, since it is important for rightly understanding what defenders of this much maligned account of the atonement are trying to say. If Christ is punished in the place of the sinner, then he takes on the harsh treatment that should be visited on the sinner, dying in their place. But there are serious objections to this idea. Two of the most serious are that it is morally wrong to seek to 'punish' an innocent person, and that the culpability for punishment does not transfer from one person to another. We would normally think that substituting someone who did not do the crime for someone who did is a gross injustice. But that is what is envisaged in the 'punishment' of Christ, who is innocent of sin. (I place the word 'punishment' in quotation marks to indicate that part of the worry here is that treating an innocent person in this way is not a punishment at all, precisely because they are *innocent*; punishment presumes guilt.)

In the case of the transference of culpability, we might distinguish between cases where a penalty might be transferred, such as the paying of a parking fine by a wealthy friend, and cases where punishment is in view. In cases of punishment of felons, for example, we would typically think that the person guilty of the crime must be the one punished. The harsh treatment they suffer cannot be transferred as it can in the case of the penalty. Part of the reason for this is that we assume in the case of most felonies that culpability attaches to the person, so it is they who must be punished. We do not have the same intuitions about penalties like parking fines. But to the extent that human sin seems more like a punishment than a penalty, we might be inclined to think that punishment must be meted out to the one guilty of the crime, not some substitute. Those who feel the force of these sorts of objections may opt instead for the more mild version of penal substitution, according to which Christ suffers only the penal consequences of human sin, not the punishment for it. Suffering the penal consequences is rather like suffering something qualitatively similar to the pains of the punishment (the harsh treatment), though it is not in fact the punishment, but a kind of surrogate for it. For, if Christ is not punished for our sin, strictly speaking, then the worries about the morality of 'punishing' an innocent, or transferring culpability, do not arise.[22]

Penal substitution and satisfaction are distinct but close relatives

Penal substitution and satisfaction are distinct but close relatives. There are other members of the same family of atonement views as well. One is the idea of Christ being a *penal example,* that is, suffering the harsh treatment that would be a punishment if it were visited on us, in order that God can demonstrate the seriousness of sin in the example of the suffering of Christ, and yet forgive us for our sin. This sort of view is often motivated by the desire to show that God, as moral governor of the universe, must ensure that human sin is treated with full moral seriousness. It is another way of trying to avoid the worries besetting the punishment version of penal substitution, and is usually called the governmental view of atonement associated with the name of the Dutch lawyer, Hugo Grotius.[23] Another close relative is *non-penal substitution*. Christ's atonement might be substitutionary in nature but not penal—relating to God's law. For it might be that Christ's atonement is a kind of vicarious act of repentance on behalf of humankind that is acted out through his life, ministry and crucifixion. This is sometimes called the *vicarious penitence view,* and is associated with the work of the Scottish nineteenth-century pastor-theologian, John Macleod Campbell.[24] It is rooted in Campbell's reading of Hebrews where we read:

> In the days of his flesh, Jesus offered up prayers and supplications, with loud cries and tears, to the one who was able to save him from death, and he was heard because of his reverent submission. Although he was a Son, he learned obedience through what he suffered; and having been made perfect, he became the source of eternal salvation for all who obey him, having been designated by God a high priest according to the order of Melchizedek. (Heb 5.7–10)

Mashups and Kaleidoscopes

There are other views besides these, and in recent times some theologians have complicated matters by attempting to provide *mashup accounts* of the atonement, which borrow elements of existing motifs and metaphors and combine them to provide a new whole composed of the parts. One good recent example of this is the work of Hans Boersma, which combines the idea of a ransom with the notion that Christ recapitulates the various stages of human life, cleansing each as he moves through them, and culminating in an atoning work that satisfies God by a penal substitutionary act of atonement.[25] Other theologians have suggested that instead of attempting mashup accounts, we should think of the atonement doctrines and motifs as capturing only one aspect of the atonement, which is too rich an idea to be limited to any one motif or idea. The atonement is like a diamond, which has many different facets. Each atonement account is like one facet of the diamond. Only when they are placed side-by-side do we see things in the round or as a whole. Similarly, only when we turn the diamond to see the different facets sparkle, do we appreciate its beauty as a whole. This sort of view is sometimes called *the kaleidoscopic approach* to the atonement, associated in particular with the work of Mark Baker and Joel Green.[26] But note that the kaleidoscopic view is not itself a doctrine of atonement. Rather, it is a way of thinking about existing views of the atonement—a kind of theory about atonement doctrines.

5 Atonement, Participation and Representation

In some recent biblical scholarship there has been quite a bit of work done on the way in which the notion of participation features in Pauline theology about atonement.[27] This is particularly true in the so-called Adam christology passages of Rom 5.12–19, and 1 Corinthians 15, where Paul compares Adam and his progeny in whose sin we participate, and Christ and his saving work, in whose work those who believe participate. How are we to understand this language? One way to think about it is to treat it with full seriousness, as implying that there is some real participation in Christ's work and its benefits brought about through union with Christ via the agency of the Holy Spirit. The Spirit is the divine person who provides the gift of faith (Ephesians 2), and who brings about the transformative experience that generates new life and a 'new creation' as Paul puts it (2 Cor 5.17). The Spirit unites us with Christ (Rom 6. 5–8; Gal 2.20, 4.6; Col 2.12–13). He enables the believer to enjoy the saving benefits of Christ's work via the gift of faith and, consequent upon this, in communion with God in Christ and in the sacraments. It is as if the Spirit's work is like someone who repairs a broken transistor in an old-fashioned radio so that the radio may once again pick up signals and be tuned in to particular programmes. The radio signals are like being united to Christ. By means of the Spirit's work we are joined with Christ, able to 'pick up' and participate in his benefits, and communion with him; and so on.

But this still leaves the question of the mechanism of atonement. If the Spirit regenerates the believer and unites them to Christ, what is the basis of this action? That is, by means of what saving work are we able to enjoy the benefits of Christ's act of reconciliation? Some recent biblical scholars have suggested that the participation of Christ in our humanity and of us in Christ is the key to understanding the means of atonement as much as it is the key to unlocking the application of the benefits of Christ's work in regeneration and union with the believer by the Spirit. But without more explanation, this seems a little vague. We want to have some idea about *how* the participation of Christ in our humanity and of us in Christ brings about atonement, if indeed it does bring about atonement.

Taking this recent literature on participation as our point of departure, I want to suggest that the atonement might be fruitfully thought of against this background Pauline participation motif as a *vicarious, reparative and penitential act of soteriological representation*—or what I shall call the *representational account of atonement* for short.[28] This is a kind of mashup view that attempts to give a layered understanding of the nature of atonement, drawing in different historic motifs into one more complex conceptual picture. The central idea is that Christ is accountable for human sin as a human (though not a sinner), but not culpable for human sin, as per traditional accounts of penal substitution. He acts on behalf of fallen humanity who cannot help themselves to salvation. In this way, his work is vicarious. He repairs the breach between God and humanity in so doing. In this way, his work is reparative. And the work itself is from beginning to end a kind of penitential act, as we have already noted with reference to the Epistle to the Hebrews. He offers a kind of penitential act on behalf of fallen humanity in his perfect life and work, culminating in his crucifixion, which pays the penalty for human sin brought about by the curse of the fall. And finally, in this work he represents humanity, being accountable for their sin. In this way, he is our representative.

Christ can be accountable without being culpable for human sin in a way similar to the parents who are accountable for the misdeed of their child, though they are not culpable for having done the misdeed themselves. In the parental case, accountability and culpability come apart. The same thing is true of the representational account of atonement. Christ is accountable but not culpable for human sin. This avoids the sort of worries we raised with traditional accounts of penal substitution. Nevertheless, on the representational view Christ's work is still performed on behalf of fallen humanity; it is still vicarious, reparative and representational. In this manner, there is much about the representational account that is like the satisfaction view of Anselm. But also present is something of the vicarious penitence account of Campbell. Christ's atonement is a penitential act made on behalf of fallen humanity, which is acceptable to God.

Christ is accountable but not culpable for human sin

Combine this with an expansive understanding of Christ's reconciling work of the sort elucidated by early Greek theologians like Athanasius or Irenaeus, where the atonement includes Christ's incarnation, life, death and resurrection. Then, Christ heals each stage of human life in his own body, representing fallen humanity, acting vicariously and penitentially. At each stage of his life he is acting in a manner consistent with God's will, living as we cannot, and ultimately paying the penalty for sin that had been set by divine fiat. But, because he is God incarnate, death may not hold him. This too recalls the image beloved of the Greek Fathers, of Christ defeating death. Even if we set to one side the metaphorical language they sometimes use that personifies death, there is something powerful about the image of Christ entering the state of death and destroying it from the inside out, so to speak.[29] In defeating death, which we might understand as Christ entering and destroying the power of death over human beings, Christ is the firstborn from the dead, the prototype of a new humanity that is not subject to the curse. Thus, the resurrection is part of the reconciling work of Christ, for it is this goal at which Christ aims, and the end awaiting redeemed human beings as well.

6
Conclusion

In this short study I have tried to give the reader a flavour of some of the contemporary debates surrounding the doctrine of atonement. It is a central Christian doctrine that has taxed some of the most important minds in history. Consequently, it is not surprising to find that in answering the question, 'What is the nature of the atonement?', we have come up against various different explanations. Should this make us despair? Not at all. But it should give us pause for thought.

The task of Christian doctrine is to help us find a conceptual framework with which to speak of the great mysteries of the faith. Hopefully, that framework will be aimed at understanding the truth of the matter, to the extent that we can fathom that truth. But, as with any human endeavour, our grip on the truth is often more fragile than we think. This is certainly true of the atonement, as we have seen. So one takeaway from our discussion of the atonement might be this: to exercise care in what we say about Christ's reconciling work, and to extend grace to others with whom we disagree on this topic. For we are all seeking to understand better the mysteries of the faith with which we have been entrusted (Jude 1.3).

Appendix: Further Reading

Introductory

Anselm of Canterbury, *Cur Deus Homo* in *Anselm: Basic Writing*, T Williams (trans) (Indianapolis, IND: Hackett, 2007) pp 237–326.

Athanasius, *On the Incarnation*, J Behr Crestwood, NJ (trans.) (Yonkers, NY: St Vladimir's Seminary Press, 2006).

G Aulén, *Christus Victor: An Historical Study of the Three Main Types of the Idea of Atonement* (London: SPCK, 1931).

J Beilby and P R Eddy (eds), *The Nature of Atonement: Four Views* (Downers Grove, IL: IVP Academic, 2006).

W L Craig, *Atonement*, Cambridge Elements in Philosophy of Religion (Cambridge University Press, 2019).

O D Crisp, *Approaching the Atonement: The Reconciling Work of Christ* (Downers Grove, IL: IVP Academic, 2020).

Gregory of Nyssa, *The Great Catechism*, in vol 5 of *The Nicene and Post-Nicene Father, Series 2*, P Schaff and H Wace (eds) (Edinburgh: T and T Clark, 1892).

L W Grensted, *A Short History of the Doctrine of Atonement* (Manchester: University of Manchester Press, 1920).

Irenaeus, *On the Apostolic Preaching*, J Behr Crestwood, NY (trans.): (Yonkers, NY: St Vladimir's Seminary Press, 1997).

A Johnson, *Atonement: A Guide for the Perplexed* (London: T and T Clark, 2015).

B Pugh, *Atonement Theories: A Way Through the Maze* (Eugene, OR: Cascade Books, 2014).

F Rutledge, *The Crucifixion: Understanding the Death of Jesus Christ* (Grand Rapids, MI: Eerdmans, 2015).

Intermediate

P Abelard, *Commentary on the Epistle to the Romans*, Fathers of the Church Medieval Continuations series, S R Cartwright (trans.) (Washington, DC: Catholic University of America Press, 2011).

M D Baker and J B Green, *Recovering the Scandal of the Cross: Atonement in New Testament and Contemporary Contexts* (Downers Grove, IL: IVP Academic, 2011).

H Boersma, *Violence, Hospitality, and the Cross: Reappropriating the Atonement Tradition* (Grand Rapids, MI: Baker Academic, 2006).

J C Brown and C R Bohn (eds), *Christianity, Patriarchy, and Abuse: A Feminist Critique* (New York: The Pilgrim Press, 1989).

Catechism of the Catholic Church, available at: https://www.vatican.va/archive/ENG0015/_INDEX.HTM (accessed 3 August 2022).

O D Crisp, *The Word Enfleshed: Exploring the Person and Work of Christ* (Grand Rapids, MI: Baker Academic, 2016).

R S Franks, *The Work of Christ* (London: Thomas Nelson, 1962).

M J Gorman, *Inhabiting the Cruciform God: Kenosis, Justification, and Theosis in Paul's Narrative Soteriology* (Grand Rapids, MI: Eerdmans, 2009).

C E Gunton, *The Actuality of Atonement: A Study of Metaphor, Rationality and the Christian Tradition* (London: T and T Clark, 1988).

J Hick, *The Metaphor of God Incarnate* (Louisville, KY: Westminster John Knox Press, 2005).

M Hooker, *From Adam to Christ: Essays on Paul* (Cambridge University Press, 1990).

A Johnson, 'Theories and *Theoria* of the Atonement: A Proposal,' *International Journal of Systematic Theology* 23.1 (2021): 92–108.

T H McCall, *Against God and Nature: The Doctrine of Sin*, Foundations of Evangelical Theology series (Wheaton, IL: Crossway, 2019).

J Miley, *The Atonement in Christ* (New York: Philips and Hunt, 1879).

B Myers, 'The Patristic Doctrine of Atonement,' in O D Crisp and F Sanders (eds), *Locating Atonement: Explorations in Constructive Dogmatics* (Grand Rapids, MI: Zondervan Academic, 2015) pp 71–88.

L Peacore, *The Role of Women's Experience in Feminist Theologies of Atonement* (Eugene, OR: Pickwick Publications, 2010).

H Rashdall, *The Idea of Atonement in Christian Theology, Being the Bampton Lectures for 1915* (London: Macmillan and Co, 1919).

J S Romanides, *The Ancestral Sin* (Ridgewood, NJ: Zephyr Publishing, 2002).

J B Stump and C Meister (eds), *Original Sin and the Fall: Five Views* (Downers Grove, IL: IVP Academic, 2020).

O T Todd, *The Moral Governmental Theory of Atonement: Re-envisioning Penal Substitution* (Eugene, OR: Cascade, 2021).

T F Torrance, *The Mediation of Christ* (Colorado Springs, CO: Helmers and Howard, 1992).

J D Weaver, *The Nonviolent Atonement* (Grand Rapids, MI: Eerdmans, 2011).

Advanced

K Anatolios, *Deification Through the Cross: An Eastern Christian Theology of Salvation* (Grand Rapids, MI: Eerdmans 2020).

J M Campbell, *The Nature of the Atonement* (1856, reprint, Grand Rapids, MI: Eerdmans, 1996).

W L Craig, *Atonement and the Death of Christ: An Exegetical, Historical, and Philosophical Exploration* (Waco, TX: Baylor University Press, 2020).

O D Crisp, *Analyzing Doctrine: Toward a Systematic Theology* (Waco, TX: Baylor University Press, 2019).

O D Crisp, *Freedom, Redemption and Communion: Studies in Christian Doctrine* (London: T and T Clark, 2021).

O D Crisp, 'Moral Exemplarism and Atonement,' *Scottish Journal of Theology* 73.2 (2020), pp 137–149.

O D Crisp, *Participation and Atonement: An Analytic and Constructive Account* (Grand Rapids, MI: Baker Academic, 2022).

O D Crisp, 'Penal non-Substitution,' *Journal of Theological Studies* NS 59 (2008), pp 140–168.

J R Farris and S M Hamilton, 'This is My Beloved Son, Whom I Hate? A Critique of the *Christus Odium* Variant of Penal Substitution,' *Journal of Biblical and Theological Studies* 3.2 (2018), pp 271–286.

H Grotius, *A Defence of the Catholic Faith Concerning the Satisfaction of Christ Against Fausus Socinus,* F H Foster (trans) (1617, reprint Andover: Warren F Draper, 1889).

A A Hodge, *The Atonement* (Philadelphia, PA: Presbyterian Board of Publication, 1867).

A Johnson (ed), *T and T Clark Companion to the Atonement* (London: T and T Clark, 2017).

D Lewis, 'Do We Believe in Penal Substitution?' *Philosophical Papers* 26 (1997), pp 203–209.

I A McFarland, *The Word Made Flesh: A Theology of the Incarnation* (Louisville, KY: Westminster John Knox, 2019).

A E McGrath, 'The Moral Theory of the Atonement: An Historical and Theological Critique,' *Scottish Journal of Theology* 38 (1985), pp 205-220.

E Stump, *Atonement,* Oxford Studies in Analytic Theology (Oxford University Press, 2018).

R Swinburne, *Responsibility and Atonement* (Oxford University Press, 1989).

K Tanner, *Christ the Key* (Cambridge University Press, 2010).

Notes

1 All biblical quotations are from the NRSV.

2 See F Rutledge, *The Crucifixion: Understanding the Death of Jesus Christ* (Grand Rapids, MI: Eerdmans, 2015).

3 See B Pugh, *Atonement Theories: A Way Through the Maze* (Eugene, OR: Cascade Books, 2014).

4 For a rather different account, which includes notions of trauma and shame, see E Stump, *Atonement,* Oxford Studies in Analytic Theology (Oxford University Press, 2018).

5 For a helpful recent overview of the doctrine of sin and original sin, see T H McCall, *Against God and Nature: The Doctrine of Sin,* Foundations of Evangelical Theology series (Wheaton, IL: Crossway, 2019); and the essays in J B Stump and C Meister (eds), *Original Sin and the Fall: Five Views* (Downers Grove, IL: IVP Academic, 2020).

6 For discussion of this Eastern Orthodox view, see J S Romanides, *The Ancestral Sin* (Ridgewood, NJ: Zephyr Publishing, 2002).

7 For a helpful overview of Roman Catholic teaching on the subject, see the *Catechism of the Catholic Church,* available online at: https://www.vatican.va/archive/ENG0015/_INDEX.HTM (last accessed 21 June 2021).

8 I have discussed this at greater length in O D Crisp, *Freedom, Redemption and Communion: Studies in Christian Doctrine* (London: T and T Clark, 2021) pp 24–49.

9 See O D Crisp, *Analyzing Doctrine: Toward a Systematic Theology* (Waco, TX: Baylor University Press, 2019); and the first chapter of O D Crisp, *Approaching the Atonement: The Reconciling Work of Christ* (Downers Grove, IL: IVP Academic, 2020).

10 Thus, S McFague. See, *eg*, her monograph *Metaphorical Theology, Models of God in Religious Language* (Philadelphia, PA: Fortress Press, 1982).

11 For recent discussion of this, see A J Johnson, 'Theories and *Theoria* of the Atonement: A Proposal,' *International Journal of Systematic Theology* 23.1 (2021), pp 92–108.

12 Athanasius, *On the Incarnation,* J Behr (trans.) (Crestwood, NJ: St Vladimir's Seminary Press, 2006) 54, 3.

13 Anselm of Canterbury, *Cur deus homo* in T Williams (trans.), *Anselm: Basic Writings* (Indianapolis, IND: Hackett, 2007) pp 237–326.

14 See T F Torrance, *The Mediation of Christ* (Colorado Springs, CO: Helmers and Howard, 1992 [1984]); K Tanner, *Christ the Key*, Current Issues in Theology (Cambridge University Press, 2010); and I A McFarland, *The Word Made Flesh: A Theology of the Incarnation* (Louisville, KY: Westminster John Knox, 2019).

15 An example of such misunderstanding can be found in A E McGrath, 'The Moral Theory of the Atonement: An Historical and Theological Critique,' *Scottish Journal of Theology* 38 (1985), pp 205–20.

16 For further discussion of this topic, see O D Crisp, 'Moral Exemplarism and Atonement,' *Scottish Journal of Theology* 73.2 (2020), pp 137–149.

17 In twentieth-century theology, Gustaf Aulén popularized the claim that the ransom view was the classic account of atonement taught by the Church Fathers. This is not a sustainable position, as any reader of Athanasius or Irenaeus will quickly discover. See Aulén, *Christus Victor: An Historical Study of the Three Main Types of the Idea of Atonement* (London: SPCK, 1931).

18 See J D Weaver, *The Nonviolent Atonement, 2nd edition* (Grand Rapids, MI: Eerdmans, 2011).

19 For a helpful recapitulation of some of the issues in this debate, see M D Baker and J B Green, *Recovering the Scandal of the Cross: Atonement in New Testament and Contemporary Contexts* (Downers Grove, IL: IVP Academic, 2nd ed, 2011) chs 2–4.

20 I do not deny that there are biblical passages that speak about God's wrath, *eg* Rom 1.18. The question is how to interpret such passages. Do we take them at face value, expressing something about the divine nature, or as analogical or even metaphorical?

21 For a contemporary defence of penal substitution that opts for the penal consequences version of the doctrine, see W L Craig, *Atonement and the Death of Christ: An Exegetical, Historical, and Philosophical Exploration* (Waco, TX: Baylor University Press, 2020). For a standard work criticizing penal substitution and other traditional atonement models, see the essays in J C Brown and C R Bohn (eds), *Christianity, Patriarchy, and Abuse: A Feminist Critique* (New York: The Pilgrim Press, 1989). For a critique of recent extreme versions of penal substitution in American conservative evangelical theology, see J R Farris and S M Hamilton, 'This is My Beloved Son, Whom I Hate? A Critique of the *Christus Odium* Variant of Penal Substitution,' *Journal of Biblical and Theological Studies* 3.2 (2018), pp 271–286.

22 A useful discussion of these issues can be found in D Lewis, 'Do We Believe in Penal Substitution?' in *Philosophical Papers* 26 (1997), pp 203–209.

23 For discussion of this view, see O D Crisp, 'Penal non-Substitution' in *Journal of Theological Studies* NS 59 (2008), pp 140–168; and O T Todd, *The Moral Governmental Theory of Atonement: Re-envisioning Penal Substitution* (Eugene, OR: Cascade, 2021).

24 See J M Campbell, *The Nature of the Atonement* (Grand Rapids, MI: Eerdmans, 1996 [1856]).

25 See H Boersma, *Violence, Hospitality, and the Cross: Reappropriating the Atonement Tradition* (Grand Rapids, MI: Baker Academic, 2006).

26 Baker and Green, *Recovering the Scandal of the Cross, op cit.*

27 See, *eg*, M J Gorman, *Inhabiting the Cruciform God: Kenosis, Justification, and Theosis in Paul's Narrative Soteriology* (Grand Rapids, MI: Eerdmans, 2009); and M Hooker, *From Adam to Christ: Essays on Paul* (Cambridge University Press, 1990).

28 This view is developed in O D Crisp, *Participation and Atonement: An Analytic and Constructive Account* (Grand Rapids, MI: Baker Academic, 2022).

29 An excellent short essay on patristic views of atonement can be found in B Myers, 'The Patristic Doctrine of Atonement,' in O D Crisp and F Sanders (eds), *Locating Atonement: Explorations in Constructive Dogmatics* (Grand Rapids, MI: Zondervan Academic, 2015) pp 71–88.